Rock It!

IDENTIFYING ROCKS

Nancy Kelly Allen

PowerKiDS press™

New York

For Sarah

Published in 2009 by The Rosen Publishing Group, Inc.
29 East 21st Street, New York, NY 10010

First Edition

Editor: Amelie von Zumbusch
Book Design: Kate Laczynski
Photo Researcher: Jessica Gerweck

Photo Credits: Cover, p. 1 © Lise Metzger/Getty Images; pp. 4, 10, 16, 18 Shutterstock.com; p. 6 © Robin Smith/Getty Images; p. 8 © Ken Lucas/Getty Images; p. 12 © Hughes Hervé/age fotostock; p. 14 © Michael Melford/Getty Images; p. 20 © Michele Westmorland/Getty Images.

Library of Congress Cataloging-in-Publication Data

Allen, Nancy Kelly, 1949–
   Identifying rocks / Nancy Kelly Allen. — 1st ed.
       p. cm. — (Rock it!)
   Includes index.
   ISBN 978-1-4358-2763-9 (library binding) — ISBN 978-1-4358-3186-5 (pbk.)
ISBN 978-1-4358-3192-6 (6-pack)
   1. Rocks—Identification—Juvenile literature. I. Title.
   QE431.5.A55 2009
   552—dc22
                                2008036035

Manufactured in the United States of America

CPSIA Compliance Information: Batch #316260PK: For further information contact Rosen Publishing, New York, New York at 1-800-237-9932.

CONTENTS

One way to get a closer look at Earth's rocks is to go for a walk or a hike, as this mother and son are doing.

One or More

Rocks are everywhere. Huge plates of rock lie under both the ground we walk on and the ocean floor. Mountains are giant blocks of rock. Sand is made of many tiny bits of rock. Earth has many kinds of rocks. Scientists separate these rocks into three groups. They are igneous rocks, metamorphic rocks, and sedimentary rocks.

Rocks are solid matter made of minerals. Minerals are nonliving, naturally occurring matter. Most rocks, such as gabbro, are made up of two or more minerals. Some rocks, such as quartzite, have only one mineral. Rocks come in many shapes, but each mineral forms **crystals** in its own special shape. For example, the mineral beryl always forms a shape with six sides.

The Remarkable Rocks, in Australia's Flinders Chase National Park, are made of an igneous rock, called granite.

6

Every Rock Has a Story

Every rock has a story to tell. Once you know a bit about rocks, you can figure out how and where a certain rock was made and what minerals it holds. Rocks even hold a record of how Earth has changed over time. The oldest rocks are **billions** of years old.

Scientists study rocks to **identify** them because different rocks have different uses and values. Shale rocks sometimes hold oil. Clay can be used to make cups and plates. **Gems**, such as rubies and emeralds, are found in some rocks. Gems are used in **jewelry** and are very expensive.

Some rocks and minerals look very much alike. People sometimes mistake pyrite for gold. Gold is an expensive mineral. Pyrite, also called fool's gold, is a mineral with less value.

Color is another property scientists use to identify minerals. Some minerals come in many colors, but azurite, seen here, is always blue.

Recognizing Minerals

Geologists, or rock scientists, group minerals by their **properties** to identify them. One such property is luster, or the way a mineral shines. For example, the mineral silver is shiny, while graphite is dull. Another important property is cleavage, or the way a mineral breaks when hit with a hammer. Flint breaks into shapes with rounded edges.

Mohs' scale is a system used to test the hardness of minerals. Ten minerals are ranked from softest to hardest. Talc is the softest mineral and diamond is the hardest. All other minerals can cut talc. However, no other minerals can cut diamonds.

Geologists also use the fizz test to study a mineral's properties. You can do a fizz test by pouring vinegar over limestone rock. This will make the rock bubble and fizz.

Granite rocks, such as the one seen here, have large grains. You can often see several different colors in a piece of granite.

Sizing Up Rocks

Scientists identify rocks by studying the kinds of minerals that make up the rocks. Geologists test the minerals' properties. These scientists look at things such as the colors, shapes, and grain sizes of the minerals in a rock.

Different kinds of rocks have different grain sizes. Some rocks, such as granite, have grains that can be seen easily. These rocks are said to have a coarse grain. Rocks such as dolerite, with grains that are small but that can still be seen with the naked eye, have a medium grain. Rocks such as rhyolite, with grains so small that they cannot be seen without a **magnifying glass**, have a fine grain.

Pumice is an unusual igneous rock.
It forms when lava hardens so quickly
that bits of air are trapped in the rock.
Pumice is so light that it floats in water!

Hot Rocks

Igneous rocks can often be identified by their shiny, grainy appearance. These rocks form when magma, or melted rock, hardens. Igneous rocks that form deep under ground, such as gabbro, have a coarse grain. This is because they cool slowly. Gabbro is usually spotted with mineral grains in bright and dark colors.

Igneous rocks that form on Earth's **surface**, such as basalt, are mostly fine grained. These rocks form when melted rock escapes through breaks in Earth's surface. Once it reaches Earth's surface, magma is called lava. Lava cools quickly. Obsidian forms when lava cools so quickly that no mineral grains form.

Lava sometimes forms tunnels of the igneous rock basalt. Idaho's Craters of the Moon National Monument has basalt tunnels that are 33 feet (10 m) wide and hundreds of feet (m) long.

You can see many layers of sedimentary rock at Reflection Canyon, in Utah. Reflection Canyon is part of Glen Canyon National Recreation Area.

Bits and Grains

Sedimentary rocks generally have larger grains than igneous rocks. Sedimentary rocks consist of matter called **sediment**. Bits of rock are one kind of sediment. Over time, **layers** of sediment build up and harden into sedimentary rock. Many sedimentary rocks have colorful layered bands. This helps scientists identify the rocks.

Many sedimentary rocks are clastic, or made of bits of rock. Those made of small, smooth rocks are called conglomerates. Breccias have bits of rock with sharp edges. Sandstones have grains of sand pressed together.

Other kinds of sediment can also become sedimentary rock. Limestone forms from the remains of sea animals. Limestone often holds the **fossilized** shells of these animals.

Amber often has fossils of animals that got stuck in tree sap inside it. Bees, lizards, and even frogs have been found trapped in amber.

16

Mineraloids

Many sedimentary rocks are made up of a mix of minerals. Other sedimentary rocks, such as halite, are minerals. Sedimentary rocks can also be mineraloids, such as amber, jet, and opal. Mineraloids do not form crystals, so they are not pure minerals.

Amber, a red or yellow mineraloid that you can see through, forms from the sap of pine trees that lived long ago. Jet is a hard, black wood fossil that is also a type of coal. Opals often form in hot springs that hold sand. Other opals form in thin layers in sedimentary rocks.

Opals may be clear, white, gray, or black. Each opal shines in a rainbow of colors. The tiny grains of sand inside the stone break up the light.

You can see the bands of minerals in these schist rocks. Metamorphic rocks whose minerals form bands are called foliated rocks.

Against the Grain

Studying a metamorphic rock's minerals is one of the best ways to identify it. Metamorphic rocks form when heat and **pressure** deep inside Earth make the minerals in rocks change. Sometimes, pressure forces the minerals in metamorphic rocks into bands. Schist forms medium-grained bands of minerals. Gneiss has bands of light and dark minerals with coarse grains. Metamorphic rocks that were made from sedimentary mudstones, such as slate, have flat or wavy lines with fine grains.

Other metamorphic rocks, such as marble and quartzite, do not form layers. Quartzite is a hard, brown, shiny rock. Pure marble is white, but marble sometimes has minerals in it that give it different colors. Silica and iron form streaks, or stripes, in marble.

Beaches are great places to find rocks. Rocks on beaches are often smooth and rounded because they have been worn down by ocean waves.

Start a Rock Collection

If you are interested in rocks, you can become a rock hound, or rock collector. Look for rocks in parks and fields, on the beach, or along streams.

You will need a few tools. Use a hammer to break rocks apart and a magnifying glass to identify mineral grains. When you break rocks, wear safety glasses to keep your eyes safe, and wrap each rock you collect in newspaper to prevent the broken pieces from flying everywhere.

Write notes about where you find each rock. The location of a rock can help you figure out what kind of rock it is. For example, breccias are generally found near cliffs.

Matching Rocks

Once you have collected some interesting rocks, you can use books called rock guides to help you identify the rocks that you have found. The first step is to look closely at the rock. Is your rock smooth or grainy? Can you see minerals in it? Does it have grains of sand?

The next step is to match your rock with those in the book. Guides provide pictures, facts, and charts to help you learn about the rocks you find. After you identify your rock, label it and read more about it.

Collecting and identifying rocks is lots of fun. You never know what stories your rocks might be able to tell you about Earth.

GLOSSARY

billions (BIL-yunz) Thousands of millions. One billion is 1,000 million.

crystals (KRIS-tulz) Pieces of hard, clear matter that have points and flat sides.

fossilized (FO-suh-lyzd) Hardened and preserved, or kept safe.

gems (JEMZ) Precious stones that may be worn as decoration.

identify (eye-DEN-tuh-fy) To tell what something is.

jewelry (JOO-ul-ree) Objects worn on the body that are made of special metals, such as gold and silver, and valued stones.

layers (LAY-erz) Thicknesses of something.

magnifying glass (MAG-nuh-fy-ing GLAS) A tool that makes something look larger than it is.

pressure (PREH-shur) A force that pushes on something.

properties (PRAH-pur-teez) Things that describe something.

sediment (SEH-deh-ment) Small bits of matter carried by wind or water.

surface (SER-fes) The outside of anything.

INDEX

WEB SITES

Due to the changing nature of Internet links, PowerKids Press has developed an online list of Web sites related to the subject of this book. This site is updated regularly. Please use this link to access the list:

www.powerkidslinks.com/rockit/identify/